Cont

CW00847386

General Knowledge

1) Portsmouth secured their first win of the 21st century when Steve Claridge scored a hat trick in a 3-0 win over which team at Fratton Park on the 29th of January 2000?

2) Portsmouth achieved back-to-back top ten finishes in the Premier League in which two seasons?

3) Who was the club's top scorer in the 2015/16 League Two season with 11 goals?

4) Who became the first Turkish player to represent the club when he made his first team debut in 2010?

5) Which goalkeeper appeared for the club aged 43 years and 1 month old in a First Division match against Manchester City in April 2002?

6) Patrick Berger scored an outrageous volley to win the BBC Goal of the Month against which team in August 2004?

7) David James saved a penalty from which Everton player as Pompy claimed a 3-0 win at Goodison Park in August 2008?

8) How many games did Portsmouth win throughout their League One relegation season in 2012/13?

9) Which team beat Pompy in the League One Play Off Semi Finals in July 2020?

10) What shirt number did John Utaka wear throughout his time at the club?

11) Who was appointed as club captain in August 2021?

12) Who scored an own goal during the 2-2 draw with Plymouth in September 2022?

13) Matty Taylor rifled in from 45 yards against Sunderland in October 2005, but who was in goal for the opposition?

14) In which year did Alexandre Gaydamak become the sole owner of Portsmouth?

15) Who scored a hat trick in the 6-2 away win over Cambridge United in February 2015?

16) Which company was the main shirt sponsor during the 2002/03 season as the team secured promotion to the Premiership?

17) Who equalised in the last minute against Newcastle in February 2004, despite being on loan from the Magpies?

18) Which team did Portsmouth face in the testimonial for Linvoy Primus in 2010?

19) Portsmouth won the First Division in the 2002/03 season, securing a final total of how many points?

20) Who scored the Premier League Goal of the Month for Portsmouth against Hull City in November 2008?

Transfers Part One

1) Who did Pompy buy from Sheffield United in March 2000?

2) Linvoy Primus arrived on a free from which team in July 2000?

3) Goalkeeper Russell Hoult was sold to which side in January 2001?

4) Peter Crouch arrived in July 2001 from which team?

5) Which player signed on a free transfer from Dynamo Zagreb in the summer of 2001?

6) Which defender was transferred to West Brom in September 2001?

7) From which team was Paul Merson signed in 2002?

8) Which midfielder signed from Spurs in the January of 2003?

9) Which goalkeeper joined after leaving Brescia in September 2003?

10) Who did Teddy Sheringham join after leaving Portsmouth in 2004?

11) Which striker was sold to Southampton in July 2005?

12) Portsmouth signed which three players from Tottenham in the 2006 January transfer window?

13) Striker Andrew Cole was brought in from which club in August 2006?

14) Who left to join Bolton in the January of 2007?

15) Who arrived from Rennes in the summer of 2007?

16) Dejan Stefanovic was sold to which team in August 2007?

17) Portsmouth purchased which defender from Spurs in August 2008?

18) Which player was sold to Real Madrid in January 2009?

19) Steve Finnan arrived at Portsmouth from which Spanish side in 2009?

20) Which 'keeper was sold to Stoke City in February 2010?

Cup Games

1) Which four teams did Portsmouth face in the Group Stage of the 2008/09 UEFA Cup?

2) Which three Pompy players missed their penalties in the shoot-out loss to Manchester United in the 2008 Community Shield?

3) Which team did Portsmouth beat 1-0 in the Quarter Final of the EFL Trophy in 2019?

4) Who scored the winning penalty as Portsmouth won the EFL Trophy in 2019?

5) Portsmouth hammered Southampton by what score in the FA Cup Fifth Round in 2010?

6) Who missed his crucial penalty before Chelsea went onto win the FA Cup Final 1-0 in 2010?

7) By what score-line did Portsmouth beat Exeter City in the Semi-Final of the EFL Trophy in February 2020?

8) Pompy were dumped out of the FA Cup in the Second Round by which team in December 2021?

9) Portsmouth set up a FA Cup Quarter Final with Arsenal in 2004 by beating which team 1-0 in their Fifth Round replay?

10) Which team knocked Portsmouth out of the League Cup in the Quarter Finals in 2005?

11) Which Manchester United player was sent off as Portsmouth claimed a memorable 1-0 victory at Old Trafford in the FA Cup Quarter Final in 2008?

12) Who scored the only goal in the FA Cup Semi Final victory over West Brom in 2008?

Memorable Games

1) By what score line did Pompy beat Cheltenham Town at home on the last day of the 2016/17 season?

2) In what year did Portsmouth record a 6-1 home win over Leicester City in The Championship?

3) Portsmouth claimed their record Premier League win by beating which team 6-1 at home in November 2003?

4) Which Reading player scored an own goal during the incredible 7-4 victory for Pompy at Fratton Park in September 2007?

5) Which side were beaten 3-0 on the last day of the 2000/01 season to ensure survival in the First Division?

6) Pompy celebrated winning the First Division title in 2003 by beating Bradford 5-0 on the final day, with which player netting a hat trick?

7) Portsmouth won a thriller 4-3 against which London club in the Premiership in August 2004?

8) Who was the Pompy manager when they beat Southampton 4-1 at home in the Premier League in April 2005?

9) Which team did Portsmouth hammer 6-0 at Fratton Park in November 2015?

10) Pedro Mendes kick started Portsmouth's survival push when he struck two wonder goals in the 2-1 win over Manchester City in March 2006, but who was the opposition goalkeeper that he beat?

Red Cards

1) Who was sent off during the 0-0 draw with Blackburn in April 2010?

2) Despite seeing Marcus Harness shown a straight red card in the first half, Portsmouth went on to beat Accrington by what score line in March 2022?

3) Portsmouth ended the game with nine men after which two players were dismissed in the 1-0 home loss to Blackburn in January 2005?

4) Who was sent off for dissent during the 2-0 Premiership loss at Fulham in November 2003?

5) What was the final score as Portsmouth and Manchester United both finished with ten men at Fratton Park in August 2007, with Sulley Muntari and Cristiano Ronaldo given their marching orders?

6) Ben Chorley was sent off for a high challenge in a 1-0 home defeat to which side in League Two in March 2014?

7) Michael Brown received two yellow cards in the 2-1 home defeat to which team in October 2009?

8) Pompy saw which two players sent off during the 3-1 defeat at Bradford in January 2002?

9) Ricardo Rocha was sent off twice in the Premier League in February 2010, against which two sides?

10) Who was sent off late on during the 2-1 home defeat to Charlton in December 2018, although his ban was later overturned?

Anagrams

Identify the players from the anagrams and the years they represented the club

1) Add Genie Rhythms
   2003-2004

2) Becalm Polls
   2006-2009

3) Raced High Rush
   2002-2011

4) Limp Ivory Sun
   2000-2009

5) Bare Trek Grip
   2003-2005

6) Shame Jet Room
   2008-2009

7) Washed Jam Ion
   2004-2012

8) Laced Livid Trot
   2011

9) Amber Wasted
   2012-2016

10) A Sand Events
    2015-2017

Managers

1) Who was appointed as Portsmouth manager in January 2000?

2) Harry Redknapp began his first spell in charge in what year?

3) What was the nationality of former manager Velimir Zajec?

4) Who replaced Tony Adams as gaffer in February 2009?

5) Who was the man in charge as Pompy lost the 2010 FA Cup Final?

6) Which team did Portsmouth lose 1-0 to in Steve Cotterill's final game in charge in October 2011?

7) Who took charge as the caretaker manager after Guy Whittingham left the club in 2013?

8) Paul Cook left Portsmouth to take charge of which club in 2017?

9) Joe Gallen took charge of one game after Kenny Jackett left in March 2021, losing 1-0 to which side?

10) What was the score against Ipswich Town in the first match under the management of the Cowley brothers?

First Goals

Can you name the team that these players scored their first goal for the club against from the options below?

1) Paul Merson
   Watford
   Middlesbrough
   Aston Villa

2) Teddy Sheringham
   West Ham
   Aston Villa
   Tottenham

3) Yakubu
   Luton Town
   Coventry City
   Grimsby Town

4) Jermain Defoe
   Chelsea
   Arsenal
   Tottenham

5) Dave Nugent
Leeds United
Liverpool
Leicester City

6) Brett Pitman
Wrexham
Rochdale
Yeovil

7) Matt Tubbs
Rochdale
Hartlepool
Rotherham

8) John Marquis
York City
Wycombe
Newport

9) Marcus Harness
Sunderland
Yeovil
Scunthorpe

10) Dane Scarlett
   Plymouth
   Port Vale
   Peterborough

Transfers Part Two

1) Portsmouth signed which player from Stoke City in September 2010?

2) Kevin Prince Boateng was sold to which side in August 2010?

3) Greg Halford arrived in July 2011 from which club?

4) Which defender was sold to Crystal Palace in May 2012?

5) Who arrived from Monaco in May 2013?

6) Who signed for Bristol City in February 2013 after leaving Pompy?

7) Which two players came in from Bristol City in the 2014 January transfer window?

8) Gavin Mahon left in January 2014 to sign for which non-league club?

9) Who signed on a free from Aston Villa in June 2015?

10) Which player was sold to Wolves in May 2015?

11) Curtis Main arrived from which club in July 2016?

12) Adam Barton was sold to which Scottish team in 2016?

13) Which striker was bought from Ipswich Town in July 2017?

14) Michael Smith left Portsmouth for which side in 2017?

15) Who joined Wigan on a free after leaving in 2018?

16) Who was bought from Shrewsbury Town in the 2019 January transfer window?

17) Recco Hackett-Fairchild was signed from which club in January 2020?

18) Who arrived on a free from Norwich City in August 2020?

19) Which two players came in from Sunderland in the 2022 January transfer window?

20) Michael Morrison moved from which team to sign for Pompy in the summer of 2022?

Answers

General Knowledge Answers

1) Portsmouth secured their first win of the 21st century when Steve Claridge scored a hat trick in a 3-0 win over which team at Fratton Park on the 29th of January 2000?
Barnsley

2) Portsmouth achieved back-to-back top ten finishes in the Premier League in which two seasons?
2006/07 and 2007/08

3) Who was the club's top scorer in the 2015/16 League Two season with 11 goals?
Gareth Evans

4) Who became the first Turkish player to represent the club when he made his first team debut in 2010?
Nadir Ciftci

5) Which goalkeeper appeared for the club aged 43 years and 1 month old in a First Division match against Manchester City in April 2002?
Dave Beasant

6) Patrick Berger scored an outrageous volley to win the BBC Goal of the Month against which team in August 2004?
Charlton Athletic

7) David James saved a penalty from which Everton player as Pompy claimed a 3-0 win at Goodison Park in August 2008?
Yakubu

8) How many games did Portsmouth win throughout their League One relegation season in 2012/13?
Ten

9) Which team beat Pompy in the League One Play Off Semi Finals in July 2020?
Oxford United

10) What shirt number did John Utaka wear throughout his time at the club?
17

11) Who was appointed as club captain in August 2021?
Clark Robertson

12) Who scored an own goal during the 2-2 draw with Plymouth in September 2022?
Sean Raggett

13) Matty Taylor rifled in from 45 yards against Sunderland in October 2005, but who was in goal for the opposition?
Kelvin Davis

14) In which year did Alexandre Gaydamak become the sole owner of Portsmouth?
2006

15) Who scored a hat trick in the 6-2 away win over Cambridge United in February 2015?
Matt Tubbs

16) Which company was the main shirt sponsor during the 2002/03 season as the team secured promotion to the Premiership?
TY Europe

17) Who equalised in the last minute against Newcastle in February 2004, despite being on loan from the Magpies?
Lomana LuaLua

18) Which team did Portsmouth face in the testimonial for Linvoy Primus in 2010?
Fulham

19) Portsmouth won the First Division in the 2002/03 season, securing a final total of how many points?
98

20) Who scored the Premier League Goal of the Month for Portsmouth against Hull City in November 2008?
Glen Johnson

Transfers Part One Answers

1) Who did Pompy buy from Sheffield United in March 2000?
Shaun Derry

2) Linvoy Primus arrived on a free from which team in July 2000?
Reading

3) Goalkeeper Russell Hoult was sold to which side in January 2001?
West Brom

4) Peter Crouch arrived in July 2001 from which team?
QPR

5) Which player signed on a free transfer from Dynamo Zagreb in the summer of 2001?
Robert Prosinecki

6) Which defender was transferred to West Brom in September 2001?
Darren Moore

7) From which team was Paul Merson signed in 2002?
Aston Villa

8) Which midfielder signed from Spurs in the January of 2003?
Tim Sherwood

9) Which goalkeeper joined after leaving Brescia in September 2003?
Pavel Srnicek

10) Who did Teddy Sheringham join after leaving Portsmouth in 2004?
West Ham

11) Which striker was sold to Southampton in July 2005?
Ricardo Fuller

12) Portsmouth signed which three players from Tottenham in the 2006 January transfer window?
Noe Pamarot, Sean Davis and Pedro Mendes

13) Striker Andrew Cole was brought in from which club in August 2006?
Manchester City

14) Who left to join Bolton in the January of 2007?
David Thompson

15) Who arrived from Rennes in the summer of 2007?
John Utaka

16) Dejan Stefanovic was sold to which team in August 2007?
Fulham

17) Portsmouth purchased which defender from Spurs in August 2008?
Younes Kaboul

18) Which player was sold to Real Madrid in January 2009?
Lassana Diarra

19) Steve Finnan arrived at Portsmouth from which Spanish side in 2009?
Espanyol

20) Which 'keeper was sold to Stoke City in February 2010?
Asmir Begovic

Cup Games Answers

1) Which four teams did Portsmouth face in the Group Stage of the 2008/09 UEFA Cup?
Wolfsburg, AC Milan, Braga and Heerenveen

2) Which three Pompy players missed their penalties in the shoot-out loss to Manchester United in the 2008 Community Shield?
Lassana Diarra, Arnold Mvuemba and Glen Johnson

3) Which team did Portsmouth beat 1-0 in the Quarter Final of the EFL Trophy in 2019?
Peterborough

4) Who scored the winning penalty as Portsmouth won the EFL Trophy in 2019?
Oliver Hawkins

5) Portsmouth hammered Southampton by what score in the FA Cup Fifth Round in 2010?
Southampton 1-4 Portsmouth

6) Who missed his crucial penalty before Chelsea went onto win the FA Cup Final 1-0 in 2010?
Kevin-Prince Boateng

7) By what score-line did Portsmouth beat Exeter City in the Semi-Final of the EFL Trophy in February 2020?
Portsmouth 3-2 Exeter City

8) Pompy were dumped out of the FA Cup in the Second Round by which team in December 2021?
Harrogate Town

9) Portsmouth set up a FA Cup Quarter Final with Arsenal in 2004 by beating which team 1-0 in their Fifth Round replay?
Liverpool

10) Which team knocked Portsmouth out of the League Cup in the Quarter Finals in 2005?
Watford

11) Which Manchester United player was sent off as Portsmouth claimed a memorable 1-0 victory at Old Trafford in the FA Cup Quarter Final in 2008?
Tomasz Kuszczak

12) Who scored the only goal in the FA Cup Semi Final victory over West Brom in 2008?
Nwankwo Kanu

Memorable Games Answers

1) By what score line did Pompy beat Cheltenham Town at home on the last day of the 2016/17 season?
Portsmouth 6-1 Cheltenham Town

2) In what year did Portsmouth record a 6-1 home win over Leicester City in The Championship?
2010

3) Portsmouth claimed their record Premier League win by beating which team 6-1 at home in November 2003?
Leeds United

4) Which Reading player scored an own goal during the incredible 7-4 victory for Pompy at Fratton Park in September 2007?
Ivar Ingimarsson

5) Which side were beaten 3-0 on the last day of the 2000/01 season to ensure survival in the First Division?
Barnsley

6) Pompy celebrated winning the First Division title in 2003 by beating Bradford 5-0 on the final day, with which player netting a hat trick?
Svetoslav Todorov

7) Portsmouth won a thriller 4-3 against which London club in the Premiership in August 2004?
Fulham

8) Who was the Pompy manager when they beat Southampton 4-1 at home in the Premier League in April 2005?
Alain Perrin

9) Which team did Portsmouth hammer 6-0 at Fratton Park in November 2015?
York City

10) Pedro Mendes kick started Portsmouth's survival push when he struck two wonder goals in the 2-1 win over Manchester City in March 2006, but who was the opposition goalkeeper that he beat?
David James

Red Cards Answers

1) Who was sent off during the 0-0 draw with Blackburn in April 2010?
Anthony Vanden Borre

2) Despite seeing Marcus Harness shown a straight red card in the first half, Portsmouth went on to beat Accrington by what score line in March 2022?
Portsmouth 4-0 Accrington

3) Portsmouth ended the game with nine men after which two players were dismissed in the 1-0 home loss to Blackburn in January 2005?
Lomano LuaLua and Amdy Faye

4) Who was sent off for dissent during the 2-0 Premiership loss at Fulham in November 2003?
Patrik Berger

5) What was the final score as Portsmouth and Manchester United both finished with ten men at Fratton Park in August 2007, with Sulley Muntari and Cristiano Ronaldo given their marching orders?
Portsmouth 1-1 Manchester United

6) Ben Chorley was sent off for a high challenge in a 1-0 home defeat to which side in League Two in March 2014?
York City

7) Michael Brown received two yellow cards in the 2-1 home defeat to which team in October 2009?
Tottenham Hotspur

8) Pompy saw which two players sent off during the 3-1 defeat at Bradford in January 2002?
Jason Crowe and Carl Tiler

9) Ricardo Rocha was sent off twice in the Premier League in February 2010, against which two sides?
Sunderland and Burnley

10) Who was sent off late on during the 2-1 home defeat to Charlton in December 2018, although his ban was later overturned?
Ben Thompson

Anagrams Answers

1) Add Genie Rhythms
   2003-2004
   Teddy Sheringham

2) Becalm Polls
   2006-2009
   Sol Campbell

3) Raced High Rush
   2002-2011
   Richard Hughes

4) Limp Ivory Sun
   2000-2009
   Linvoy Primus

5) Bare Trek Grip
   2003-2005
   Patrik Berger

6) Shame Jet Room
   2008-2009
   Jerome Thomas

7) Washed Jam Ion
   2004-2012
   Jamie Ashdown

8) Laced Livid Trot
   2011
   David Cotterill

9) Amber Wasted
   2012-2016
   Adam Webster

10) A Sand Events
    2015-2017
    Enda Stevens

Managers Answers

1) Who was appointed as Portsmouth manager in January 2000?
Tony Pulis

2) Harry Redknapp began his first spell in charge in what year?
2002

3) What was the nationality of former manager Velimir Zajec?
Croatian

4) Who replaced Tony Adams as gaffer in February 2009?
Paul Hart

5) Who was the man in charge as Pompy lost the 2010 FA Cup Final?
Avram Grant

6) Which team did Portsmouth lose 1-0 to in Steve Cotterill's final game in charge in October 2011?
Leeds United

7) Who took charge as the caretaker manager after Guy Whittingham left the club in 2013?
Andy Awford

8) Paul Cook left Portsmouth to take charge of which club in 2017?
Wigan Athletic

9) Joe Gallen took charge of one game after Kenny Jackett left in March 2021, losing 1-0 to which side?
Peterborough

10) What was the score against Ipswich Town in the first match under the management of the Cowley brothers?
Portsmouth 2-1 Ipswich

First Goals Answers

1) Paul Merson
   Watford

2) Teddy Sheringham
   Aston Villa

3) Yakubu
   Grimsby Town

4) Jermain Defoe
   Chelsea

5) Dave Nugent
   Leeds United

6) Brett Pitman
   Rochdale

7) Matt Tubbs
   Hartlepool

8) John Marquis
   York City

9) Marcus Harness
    Sunderland

10) Dane Scarlett
    Port Vale

Transfers Part Two Answers

1) Portsmouth signed which player from Stoke City in September 2010?
Dave Kitson

2) Kevin Prince Boateng was sold to which side in August 2010?
Genoa

3) Greg Halford arrived in July 2011 from which club?
Wolves

4) Which defender was sold to Crystal Palace in May 2012?
Joel Ward

5) Who arrived from Monaco in May 2013?
Romain Padovani

6) Who signed for Bristol City in February 2013 after leaving Pompy?
Brian Howard

7) Which two players came in from Bristol City in the 2014 January transfer window?
Nicky Shorey and Ryan Taylor

8) Gavin Mahon left in January 2014 to sign for which non-league club?
Tamworth

9) Who signed on a free from Aston Villa in June 2015?
Enda Stevens

10) Which player was sold to Wolves in May 2015?
Jed Wallace

11) Curtis Main arrived from which club in July 2016?
Doncaster Rovers

12) Adam Barton was sold to which Scottish team in 2016?
Partick Thistle

13) Which striker was bought from Ipswich Town in July 2017?
Brett Pitman

14) Michael Smith left Portsmouth for which side in 2017?
Bury

15) Who joined Wigan on a free after leaving in 2018?
Kai Naismith

16) Who was bought from Shrewsbury Town in the 2019 January transfer window?
Bryn Morris

17) Recco Hackett-Fairchild was signed from which club in January 2020?
Bromley

18) Who arrived on a free from Norwich City in August 2020?
Sean Raggett

19) Which two players came in from Sunderland in the 2022 January transfer window?
Denver Hume and Aiden O'Brien

20) Michael Morrison moved from which team to sign for Pompy in the summer of 2022?
Reading

If you enjoyed this book please consider leaving a five star review on Amazon

Books by Jack Pearson available on Amazon:

Cricket:

The Quiz Book of the England Cricket Team in the 21st Century
Cricket World Cup 2019 Quiz Book
The Ashes 2019 Cricket Quiz Book
The Ashes 2010-2019 Quiz Book
The Ashes 2005 Quiz Book
The Indian Premier League Quiz Book

Football:

The Quiz Book of Premier League Football Transfers
The Quiz Book of the England Football Team in the 21st Century
The Quiz Book of Arsenal Football Club in the 21st Century
The Quiz Book of Aston Villa Football Club in the 21st Century
The Quiz Book of Chelsea Football Club in the 21st Century

The Quiz Book of Everton Football Club in the 21st Century

The Quiz Book of Leeds United Football Club in the 21st Century

The Quiz Book of Leicester City Football Club in the 21st Century

The Quiz Book of Liverpool Football Club in the 21st Century

The Quiz Book of Manchester City Football Club in the 21st Century

The Quiz Book of Manchester United Football Club in the 21st Century

The Quiz Book of Newcastle United Football Club in the 21st Century

The Quiz Book of Southampton Football Club in the 21st Century

The Quiz Book of Sunderland Association Football Club in the 21st Century

The Quiz Book of Tottenham Hotspur Football Club in the 21st Century

The Quiz Book of West Ham United Football Club in the 21st Century

The Quiz Book of Wrexham Association Football Club in the 21st Century

Printed in Great Britain
by Amazon

34662360R00036